Kangaroos Have Joeys

by Emily J. Dolbear and E. Russell Primm

Animals and Their Young

Content Adviser: Terrence E. Young Jr., M.Ed., M.L.S.
Jefferson Parish (La.) Public Schools, and Janann Jenner, Ph D.

Reading Adviser: Dr. Linda D. Labbo,
Department of Reading Education, College of Education,
The University of Georgia

COMPASS POINT BOOKS

Minneapolis, Minnesota

Compass Point Books
3722 West 50th Street, #115
Minneapolis, MN 55410

Visit Compass Point Books on the Internet at *www.compasspointbooks.com* or e-mail your request to *custserv@compasspointbooks.com*

Photographc ©: Hans Reinhard/Bruce Coleman, Inc., cover; Daniel J. Cox/naturalexposures.com, 4; Erwin C. "Bud" Nielsen/Visuals Unlimited, 6; Jen and Des Bartlett/Bruce Coleman, Inc. 8, 16; Roger A. Powell/Visuals Unlimited, 10; Mark Newman/Bruce Coleman, Inc., 12; M.H. Tierney Jr./Visuals Unlimited, 14; Tom Brakefield/Bruce Coleman, Inc., 18; Joe McDonald/Bruce Coleman, Inc., 20.

Editors: E. Russell Primm and Emily J. Dolbear
Photo Researcher: Svetlana Zhurkina
Photo Selector: Linda S. Koutris
Designer: Bradfordesign, Inc.

Library of Congress Cataloging-in-Publication Data

Dolbear, Emily J.
    Kangaroos have joeys / by Emily J. Dolbear and E. Russell Primm III.
        p. cm. — (Animals and their young)
    Includes bibliographical references (p.   ).
    ISBN 0-7565-0061-3 (hardcover : lib. bdg.)
        1. Kangaroos—Infancy—Juvenile literature. [1. Kangaroos. 2. Animals—Infancy.] I. Primm, E. Russell, 1958– . II. Title. III. Series.
QL737.M35 D65 2001
599.2'22—dc21
                                                                                    00-011503

Table of Contents

What Are Joeys?

Baby kangaroos are called **joeys**. Mother kangaroos carry their joeys in a pouch on their bellies, just like koala bears do. (Male kangaroos have no pouch.)

Most kangaroos live in Australia. There are many kinds of kangaroos. The main kinds are gray kangaroos, red kangaroos, wallabies, and rat kangaroos.

Wallabies are one kind of kangaroo.

What Happens before Joeys Are Born?

A mother kangaroo gives birth about one month after mating with a male kangaroo. A few days before her joey is born, she licks her pouch clean for the new baby.

The mother kangaroo gives birth to only one joey a year. But she can take care of more than one joey at a time. Joeys stay with their mother until they can take care of themselves.

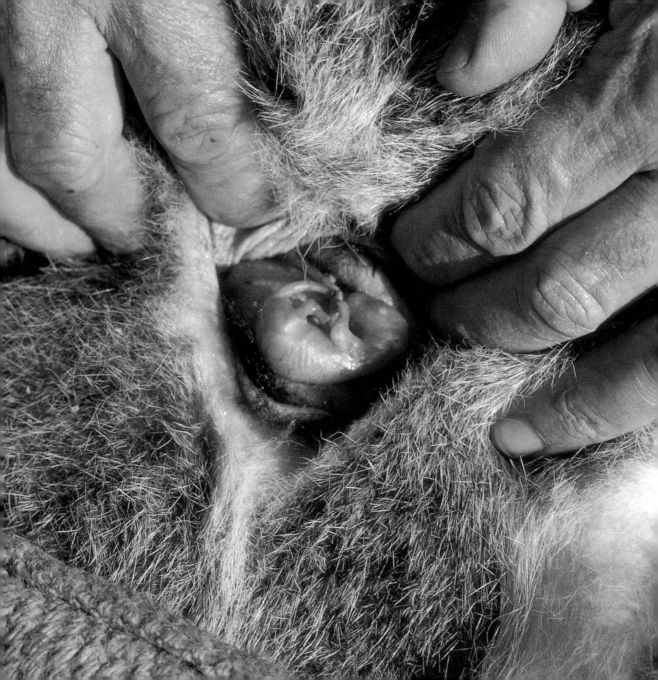

What Happens after Joeys Are Born?

A newborn joey is pink, hairless, and only about 1 inch (2.5 centimeters) long. It weighs about as much as a paper clip—0.03 ounce (1 gram). Its eyes are closed at birth and it can't hear. But, within seconds after birth, the joey uses its front legs to climb up its mother's fur to her pouch.

Kangaroos are called **marsupials.** This is the Latin word for "pouch." Koala bears, opossums, and wombats are also marsupials.

A tiny joey inside its mother's pouch

How Do Joeys Feed?

Inside the mother kangaroo's pouch are four **teats**, or nipples. The joey gets its mother's milk from these teats. It latches onto a teat as soon as it reaches the mother's pouch. The teat swells. The joey becomes a part of the teat. Muscles in the teat push the milk into the joey's mouth. The joey is on the teat for about seventy days.

A joey **nurses**, or drinks milk from its mother, right after it is born. It knows how to nurse without being taught. This is called **instinct**.

When joeys get bigger, they nurse outside their mother's pouch.

What Does a Joey Look Like?

A newborn joey looks more like a bean than a kangaroo. But when it is older, a joey looks like a smaller version of its parents. A joey has a small head and large ears. It has two short front legs and two long back legs. The front feet have five toes and the back feet have four.

A joey also has a long, thick tail. This strong tail helps kangaroos to keep their balance when they hop or stand.

Joeys grow to look exactly like their parents.

What Colors Are Joeys?

Joeys are usually gray, red, or brown. Male red kangaroos have red fur. Female red kangaroos have blue-gray fur.

The color of the kangaroo's fur helps it blend into the dry grasslands and deserts. This protects it from its enemies. Foxes and wild dogs called dingoes attack kangaroos.

A red kangaroo with her joey

What Do Joeys Do and Eat?

After about 235 days in its mother's pouch, a joey begins to wiggle around. At first it just peeps out of the pouch. Then it leaves the pouch for only a minute. Sometimes it falls out! As it grows older, the joey spends more time outside the pouch.

Older joeys play with one another and sleep a lot. At night, they look for food. They eat mostly plants and bushes. Of course, joeys also need water. This isn't always easy to find in the dry grasslands of Australia.

◀ It can be hard for kangaroos to find drinking water in Australia.

What Happens As a Joey Grows Older?

Joeys grow into quick, powerful animals. Red kangaroos can hop as fast as 30 miles (48 kilometers) an hour. They use their back feet to jump as high as 6 feet (1.8 meters). And they can travel almost that far in a single hop.

Some kangaroos live in groups called **mobs**. The strongest male is the leader of the group. He is called a **boomer**. Angry kangaroos are dangerous. If they are attacked, they kick with their strong back legs.

◀ A kangaroo's strong legs and long tail help it jump long distances.

When Is a Joey Grown Up?

A grown-up joey leaves its mother's pouch forever when it is about one year old. Adult male kangaroos weigh about 100 pounds (45 kilograms). Females always weigh less than the males. The largest kangaroo is the male red kangaroo. He weighs up to 200 pounds (91 kilograms).

Red kangaroos usually live twelve to eighteen years. Some kangaroos live as long as twenty-four years! Sadly, kangaroos don't often reach that age in the wild. Many die because of the lack of water. Hunters kill many others.

An adult male red kangaroo can weigh as much as a man.

Glossary

boomer—the strongest male in a group of kangaroos

instinct—a natural behavior; knowing what to do without being taught

joeys—young kangaroos

marsupials—a group of animals whose babies develop in a pouch on the mother's belly

mobs—groups of kangaroos

nurse—to drink milk produced by the mother

teats—nipples on the mother's body where the young can suck milk

Did You Know?

- Kangaroos are the largest marsupials.

- Kangaroos can swim.

- In Australia, road signs warn drivers about kangaroo crossings.

Want to Know More?

At the Library

Crewe, Sabrina. *The Kangaroo*. Austin, Tex.: Raintree Steck-Vaughn, 1997.

Lepthien, Emilie U. *Kangaroos*. Chicago: Children's Press, 1995.

Markle, Sandra. *Outside and Inside Kangaroos*. New York: Atheneum, 1999.

On the Web

Kangaroos Trivia and Facts

http://www.funtrivia.com/Animals/Kangaroos.html

For fun facts and trivia about kangaroos

Kangaroos at the Australian A-Z Animal Archive

http://www.aaa.com.au/A_Z/K.shtml

For general information about kangaroos and other animals from Australia

Through the Mail

The Marsupial Society of Australia, Inc.

G.P.O. Box 2462

Adelaide, S.A. 5001 Australia

To order games and puzzles about marsupials

On the Road

Kangaroo Conservation Center

222 Bailey-Waters Road

Dawsonville, GA 30534

706/265-6100

To visit a working animal farm with the most kangaroos outside of Australia

Index

About the Authors

Emily J. Dolbear has been an editor for Franklin Watts, Children's Press, and The Ecco Press. She now works as a freelance writer and editor. Dolbear lives in Chicago with her husband and son.

E. Russell Primm has worked as an editor for more than twenty years. He has been editorial director for Ferguson Publishing Company and for Children's Press and Franklin Watts. He now heads Editorial Directions, a book-producing and consulting company. He lives in Chicago.